W9-BYW-314

WITHDRAWN FROM
COLLECTION

An orchestra of toads or frogs was believed
to accompany the Mayan rain god Chaac,
because their croaking could call forth
the rain.

© 2007 Rourke Publishing LLC

All rights reserved. No part of this book may be reproduced or utilized in any form or by any means, electronic or mechanical including photocopying, recording, or by any information storage and retrieval system without permission in writing from the publisher.

www.rourkepublishing.com

Editor: Frank Sloan

How The Peacock Got Its Feathers is based on a Mayan tale from El Salvador included in *El Alma Misteriosa del Mayab* by Luis Rosada Vega, 1957

To Farrah, with love
  -S.S.

Library of Congress Cataloging-in-Publication Data

Sepehri, Sandy.
  How the peacock got its feathers : based on a Mayan tale / retold by Sandy Sepehri ; illustrated by Brian Demeter.
     p. cm. -- (Latin American tales and myths)
  ISBN 1-60044-143-2
  1. Mayas--Folklore. 2. Tales--Central America. 3. Peafowl--Folklore. I. Demeter, Brian. II. Title. III. Series.
  F1435.3.F6S46 2007
  398.208997'42--dc22
                        2006014828

Printed in the USA

How The Peacock Got Its Feathers

Based On A Mayan Tale

Retold by Sandy Sepehri
Illustrated by Brian Demeter
Cover design and storyboards
by Nicola Stratford
Project Consultant:
Silvina Peralta Ramos

Rourke
Publishing LLC
Vero Beach, Florida 32964

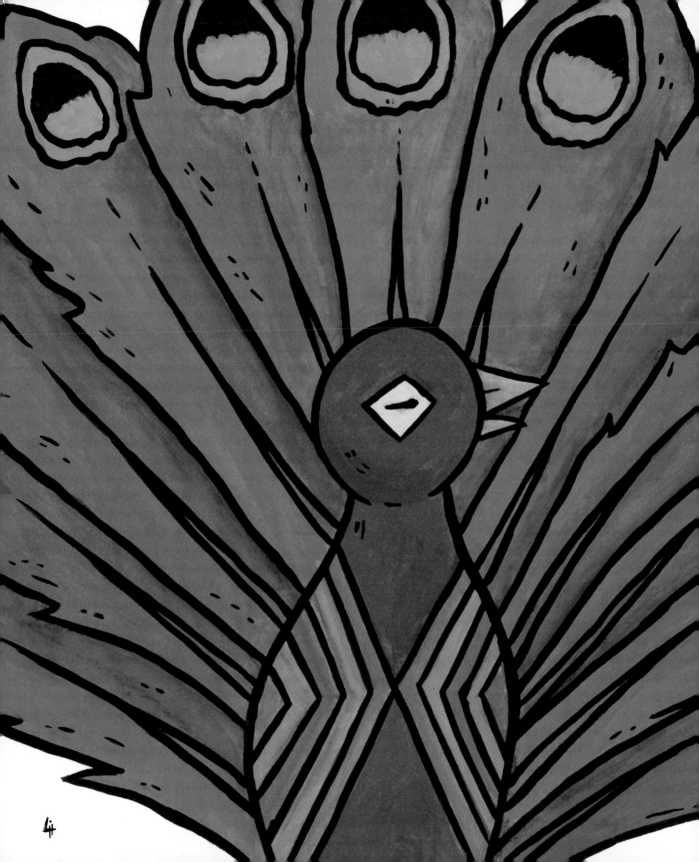

One of the most beautiful animals in the world is the peacock. His tall body is bright blue and his tail is a magnificent fan of long wispy feathers. But, say the **Mayan** Indians of **El Salvador**, he was not always so beautiful.

Long ago the male peacock was as drab as the female, the peahen, who is as dull and colorless as a rainy day. Instead, **Chaac**, the Mayan rain god in charge of animals, gave the peahen a wonderful singing voice. The peahen was proud of her voice, but she wanted a coat of brilliant colors.

One day, Chaac came down to Earth to hold a meeting with all the birds. He had a glorious **headdress** of long, shining feathers woven of gold, silk, and rainbows.

"My friends," Chaac said to all the gathered birds, "it is time to choose a new ruler. King Eagle has performed well for many years. Let us all cheer him for the wonderful job he has done."

All the birds let out a chorus of chirps and tweets of gratitude for King Eagle. Then they began chirping about choosing a new leader.

"I should be leader," hooted the owl. "My wisdom will make me a good king."

"Wisdom is not enough," screeched the falcon. "A good king should be able to fly high and see far distances to know what is happening."

Chaac became impatient with all the chirping and screeching.

MORTON MANDAN PUBLIC LIBRARY

"You shall vote tomorrow," said Chaac, "and choose wisely. A ruler must be good at many things. He must help those who are weak to find food and shelter. Most of all, he must put the needs of his fellow birds before his own."

Then Chaac flew up into the sky. He disappeared behind the clouds, and then the gathering of birds followed and flew off in their own directions.

Unlike her fellow birds, the peahen hardly listened to a word Chaac was saying. Next to wanting beautiful feathers, she wanted to be ruler of all the birds.

Maybe if she had those feathers, all the birds would vote for her. She thought she knew where to find beautiful feathers. She flapped her gray wings and flew after Chaac.

Just as it was getting dark, the peahen reached Chaac's house and landed on his windowsill. She watched Chaac remove his headdress and lie down to sleep. She saw the feathers in his headdress.

"Those are the feathers I must have," she decided. So, diving at the headdress like a buzzard after a **carcass,** she snatched the feathers. With the headdress firmly in her beak, she dashed to the window and flew away.

Although the headdress was heavy, the peahen thought how beautiful she would look in her new feathers!

When she reached home she laid the headdress on the grass and marveled at its glory. "With my singing voice and these feathers, I will be the greatest ruler these birds have ever known."

To the peahen the headdress was enormous. Her tiny head slipped right through it, and the headdress slid down. She tried walking, but stumbled over the long feathers and fell on her face.

She finally shifted the headdress over her body until it sloped down to her tail. She hoisted up the feathers in a high fan and opened them with great **panache**. Her shuffling made a few feathers break loose and fall to the ground.

Not wanting any of the feathers to go to waste, she picked them up and put them on her head like a bird tiara.

"How magnificent I look," she gushed and hurried to the election ceremony.

All the birds had gathered there, just as Chaac had directed them to. They chattered about whom they should elect as their new leader.

Suddenly the birds heard lovely music in the distance. The sound came closer and closer, and the birds were **mesmerized** by it.

Into the clearing strutted the peahen in her feathers. "This bird is so beautiful," cried the cardinal. "Surely our new ruler should be beautiful."

"Only one bird—the peacock—recognized her for who she really was. He knew her wonderful singing voice, but her tail feathers were completely strange. In fact, the feathers did not resemble those of any bird he had ever seen.

"She has stolen those feathers and I know from whom!" shouted the peacock. He flew off to Chaac's palace, and there he found Chaac looking all over his room for his headdress.

Chaac looked up and saw the humble peacock in his doorway.

"I am sorry to say," said the peacock, "that your headdress has been stolen by my mate, and she is wearing the feathers on her rear end!"

"Is that so?" asked Chaac, laughing at the thought of his headdress upon the peahen's bottom.

Peacock continued. "She is using your feathers and her singing voice to persuade the birds to elect her their new ruler. She is tricking the other birds."

"We must do something about this," said Chaac. He extended his arm for the peacock to perch on. Together they descended to the ground, and all the birds bowed down to him in respect.

When she saw Chaac, the peahen stopped singing.

"Peahen," called Chaac, "do you really think my feathers will make you a good ruler?"

"Well…" the peahen stammered. "I have a beautiful singing voice and now I have feathers to match."

Stealing his headdress was bad enough, thought Chaac. And now she was criticizing his judgment for giving her a simple coat of feathers. And she had done this in a rude, **impertinent** manner. Chaac was very angry.

"Foolish fowl!" shouted Chaac. "Beauty is not a coat you can put on! True beauty is something on the inside, and it rises to the surface from that creature's good deeds."

Then Chaac turned to the crowd of birds. "I would like to say my friend Peacock would make an excellent new ruler. He was not fooled by Peahen."

Then all the birds cheered for the peacock.

"As a token of my appreciation," said Chaac, "I will bestow upon you my own headdress."

"Peahen," shouted Chaac, "remove my feathers and give them to your new ruler."

Then Peahen wriggled out of her fancy costume and placed it on the peacock.

"From now on," said Chaac to the peahen, "you will have to earn the respect of others through your kindness, not your singing." And he took away her singing voice.

Because the peacock was such an honorable ruler, Chaac decided that every peacock from that time on would have such a tail of feathers. And so it happened.

To this day the peacock is known for his dazzling beauty. The peahen, however, can now only screech and squawk.

She learned her lesson and has never tried to steal anyone else's feathers.

Glossary

carcass (CAR kiss) – the body of a dead animal

Chaac (ch AAHK) – the Mayan rain god, often portrayed with an elephant tusk nose and accompanied by an orchestra of frogs. This god was a very important deity in a Mayan society, which depended on agriculture

El Salvador (el SAL vah door) – a nation in Central America, equal in area and population to the state of Massachusetts.

headdress (HEAD DRES) – a decorative covering for the head

impertinent (im PER tin ent) – rude and improper

Mayan (MY yen) Indians – probably the best-known of the classical civilizations of Mesoamerica, originating in the Yucatán around 2600 B.C. The Mayans developed astronomy, calendar systems, and hieroglyphic writing and are noted for their elaborate architecture, including temple-pyramids, palaces, and observatories, all built without metal tools.

mesmerized (MEZ mer EYZED) – hypnotized

panache (pan ASH) – flamboyance in style and action

About The Author

Sandy Sepehri lives with her husband, Shahram, and their three children in Florida. She has a bachelor's degree and writes freelance articles and children's stories.